W9-ABH-420

CAREER EXPLORATION

Graphic Designer

by Lewann Sotnak

Consultant:
John M. DuFresne, AIGA
Chair, Visual Communications
College of Visual Arts, St. Paul

CAPSTONE BOOKS

an imprint of Capstone Press
Mankato, Minnesota

Capstone Books are published by Capstone Press
P.O. Box 669, 151 Good Counsel Drive, Mankato, Minnesota 56002
http://www.capstone-press.com

Library of Congress Cataloging-in-Publication Data
Sotnak, Lewann.
    Graphic designer/by Lewann Sotnak.
    p. cm.—(Career exploration)
    Includes bibliographical references and index.
    Summary: An introduction to the career of graphic designer, including
discussion of educational requirements, duties, workplace, salary, employment
outlook, and possible future positions.
    ISBN 0-7368-0328-9
    1. Graphic arts—Juvenile literature. 2. Graphic arts—Vocational guidance—
Juvenile literature. [1. Graphic arts—Vocational guidance. 2. Occupations.
3. Vocational guidance.] I. Title. II. Series.
NC1001.S68 2000
741.6'023—dc21   99-28599
                                                              CIP

Editorial Credits
Leah K. Pockrandt, editor; Steve Christensen, cover designer; Kia Bielke, illustrator;
    Heidi Schoof, photo researcher

Photo Credits
International Stock/Mark Bolster, 10; Richard Hackett, 13; Scott Barrow, 25 (top);
    Ryan Williams, 25 (bottom); Jay Thomas, 32; Julian Cotton, 38
Nancy Ferguson, 41
Photo Network/Chad Ehlers, 14, 29; Jeff Greenberg, 20; Douglas Pulsigher, 35;
    Mike Moreland, 46
Unicorn Stock Photos/Eric R. Berndt, 6; Unicorn Stock Photos, 17; Unicorn Stock
    Photos/Arni Katz, 19; Tom McCarthy, 23; Steve Bourgeois, 26
Uniphoto, cover, 9
Visuals Unlimited/Jeff Greenberg, 36

**Thank you to Dan Poppie, a graphic designer with Benyas AD Group Inc. of
Minneapolis, for his assistance in preparing this book.**

Table of Contents

Fast Facts

Career Title	Graphic Designer
O*NET Number	334058B
DOT Cluster (Dictionary of Occupational Titles)	Professional, technical, and managerial occupations
DOT Number	141.061-018
GOE Number (Guide for Occupational Exploration)	01.02.03
NOC Number (National Occupational Classification-Canada)	5241
Salary Range (U.S. Bureau of Labor Statistics, Human Resources Development Canada, and other industry sources, late 1990s figures)	U.S.: $14,560 to $110,000 Canada: $14,500 to $100,000 (Canadian dollars)
Minimum Educational Requirements	U.S.: associate's degree or bachelor's degree Canada: diploma or bachelor's degree
Registration Requirements	U.S.: none Canada: varies by province

Subject Knowledge	Computers and electronics; design; fine arts; telecommunications; communications and media
Personal Abilities/Skills	Understand and apply artistic principles and skills; imagine how the final product will look from rough sketches or work drawings; use art tools; produce accurate images for displays or scenery; produce illustrations for written materials or works of art; choose the proper equipment to express an idea or create a particular effect
Job Outlook	U.S.: faster than average growth Canada: good
Personal Interests	Artistic: interest in creating ways to show feelings or ideas
Similar Types of Jobs	Visual artist; exhibition designer; environmental designer; package designer; publication designer; art director; interactive designer; illustrator; commercial artist; graphic artist; typographer

Chapter 1

Graphic Designer

Graphic designers create visual images to inform, entertain, or persuade people. These images also are called graphics. Designers use artistic skills and tools such as computers to create these graphics. Graphic designers sometimes are called visual artists. In Canada, graphic designers also are called visual communication designers.

What Graphic Designers Do

Graphic designers create designs to meet the needs of clients. Those who use the services of designers include companies, businesses, organizations, and individuals.

Graphic designers arrange words and art on pages or products. This arrangement also is called a layout. Words in layouts are called copy. Designers may work on magazines, newspapers,

Graphic designers arrange words and art in layouts.

7

books, or other publications. They also may design brochures. These pamphlets advertise a company's products or services. Some designers work on billboards, advertisements, packages, or logos. A logo is a symbol that represents a company or organization. Others may design new images for computer software, compact disks, or other computer products.

Graphic designers can work on a variety of projects. For example, they may design book covers for publishers. They may add graphics to reports and other printed business materials. Designers also create signs, shopping bags, and games for companies. They also may design graphics for TV programs or stations.

Some graphic designers work closely with other artists and writers. These people create artwork for a variety of purposes. Designers work with illustrators and photographers to create products such as posters, T-shirts, and calendars. Designers may work with writers on advertisements and other materials for companies and businesses.

Tools Used by Graphic Designers

Most graphic designers work on computers. Computers give graphic designers many

Most graphic designers work on computers.

advantages. Designers can easily correct their mistakes and make changes using computers. Designers can do more work in less time on computers. Designers use different computer programs for their jobs. Computer programs allow graphic designers many creative options.

Designers often use computer scanners. These machines make electronic copies of artwork that can be viewed on computer monitors. Designers scan pictures or designs into their computers. They can alter and enlarge images with computer

Graphic designers can alter saved computer images at a later time.

programs. The images may be stored in the computers. Designers can save these images to use or alter at a later time.

Some designers create photography layouts. These designers may use photographs taken with regular cameras or digital cameras. Digital cameras do not use film like regular cameras do. They store electronic images on computer disks instead. The images can be viewed, altered, and printed using computers.

Graphic designers also use standard art tools. These include colored pencils or pens, rulers, and color charts. Designers also may use a loupe to select photographs and proof printing. This small magnifying glass allows designers to look closely at small items.

Where Graphic Designers Work
Graphic designers work in different settings. Many designers specialize in a particular area of design.

Most graphic designers work in design studios. They help the public learn about their clients' businesses, organizations, or products. These designers produce items such as web pages, logos, brochures, and posters.

Some graphic designers work for advertising agencies. These businesses create advertisements for companies and other clients. Designers at advertising agencies also are called art directors. They work with artists and writers at the agencies to create advertising campaigns for their clients. These plans may include print, TV, radio, and Internet advertisements.

Some graphic designers work as in-house graphic designers for companies, public institutions, or organizations. These include hospitals, banks, universities, and government agencies. In-house designers create materials that promote the companies, institutions, or organizations. These materials include brochures, advertisements, newsletters, and logos.

Some graphic designers are freelancers. These designers do not work for firms or companies. They own their own businesses. Some freelancers have home studios. Freelancers provide design services for many clients. Clients may include advertising agencies, studios, or other design businesses that need extra help.

Freelancers charge their clients fees for their services. The fees may vary with each job. Freelance designers must find their own clients. Experienced freelancers may have many regular clients.

Employment
Graphic designers may work in a variety of settings. Graphic designers work for companies, retail stores, public institutions, organizations, or design firms.

Graphic designers meet with their clients to discuss designs and ideas.

Many freelance designers work near their clients. This allows designers to meet with their clients more easily than if they lived far away. Clients also are able to check on the progress of designs. Some designers may work farther away. Technology and equipment such as the Internet and fax machines provide opportunities for such arrangements.

Chapter 2

A Day on the Job

Graphic designers can work in many types of jobs. They may be publication, advertising, packaging, or web page designers. They also may be layout artists. Designers have busy schedules. They may perform a variety of duties throughout the day. They also may meet with clients, artists, and other designers.

Graphic Designers at Work
In the morning, graphic designers may have creative meetings. These meetings usually involve designers, managers, and co-workers. People at these meetings may share ideas about designs or project assignments. They discuss the progress and deadlines of projects. A deadline is the time a project must be finished.

Graphic designers meet with designers, managers, and co-workers in creative meetings.

Designers and co-workers also may schedule other appointments at creative meetings.

Graphic designers work on projects the rest of the day. They may research information for projects. This research can include talking to clients. Designers also may meet with vendors. These companies or individuals sell goods or services to businesses or companies.

During the day, graphic designers may work on parts of several projects. For example, they may work on overview sketches for proposed projects. This work includes providing ideas for advertisements or other materials. Designers or creative teams need to show their ideas to clients before they proceed with projects. They may make mock-ups to show their clients. These full-sized design proposals allow clients to see different ideas.

Graphic designers help select photographs and other graphic elements for their designs. They may select sites for photographers to take photographs. Designers also may direct photographers at photo shoots. Designers often

Graphic designers may direct photographers at photo shoots.

tell photographers how they would like photographs taken. For example, designers may tell photographers how they want products and people to appear in photographs.

Most graphic designers work for businesses or companies. They usually have standard office hours. But they may work extra hours to meet deadlines.

Layout Artists

Some graphic designers work as layout artists.
These people create page or product designs.
They use copy, graphics, and other art elements
in their designs. Art elements include borders and
background colors.

Designers must put together layouts that are
pleasing. Layouts must attract readers. Designers
need to get their clients' messages across quickly.
Most clients want attractive layouts that are not
cluttered. The material must be organized. This
helps readers understand the material.

Publication Designers

Some graphic designers work at companies
that publish books, magazines, or newspapers.
Designers at publishing companies decide on the
size and style of print in books. They also decide
how photographs or other artwork will be used.

Magazines and newspapers need layouts that
work with many photos and a great deal of copy.
Graphic designers use different print sizes. They
arrange copy in different ways. Designers also
may use shadows or colors in layouts. They use

Layout artists try to create attractive layouts.

artwork and photos in different shapes and sizes. Different features make pages look interesting to readers.

Graphic design teams may create icons for use in publications. These symbols and designs are used with certain features of publications. These may include special sections or comics. Icons help readers find their favorite features quickly.

Packaging designers must learn what package aspects appeal to people.

Icons also help readers identify certain sections of books, magazines, or newspapers.

Advertising Designers
Advertising designers must meet with clients to discuss what the clients want. Designers discover which messages clients want to share. They also find out what audiences the clients want to reach. These people are the clients' target audiences.

Advertising designers imagine ways to express clients' ideas visually. Designers consider using various colors, styles, prints, and illustrations.

Advertising designers may meet with creative teams. Team members discuss the designers' ideas. They also discuss what kind of art and copy to use. Teams also may include copywriters. A copywriter writes copy for layouts.

Designers continue to work on projects. They decide which suggestions to use. They also may work with illustrators and photographers.

Advertising designers then show their ideas to their clients. Clients do not always like designers' ideas. Designers work with clients to find designs that the clients like. Clients must approve the designs before projects can be printed or produced.

Packaging Designers

Other graphic designers create packages for products. These designers consult with clients to find out different features of the packaging. Designers learn who will buy or use the products. They learn which colors, shapes, and designs appeal to these target audiences. This knowledge helps designers create packaging.

Graphic designers want buyers to notice their packages. They use simple messages and make sure company logos are visible. Designers arrange copy and images. They also may add colors, borders, or other designs.

Packaging designers must make sure product information is easily visible. For example, toy packages must be labeled if the products are suitable for older or younger children.

Web Page Designers

Some graphic designers create web sites for clients. Web designers arrange the elements for web pages on the Internet. These elements include photos, copy, illustrations, and colors. Graphics are part of the overall look of web pages. Web page designers must design web sites that will suit the Internet users. Designers must understand the needs of web site users and clients.

Web page designers may work for various types of businesses. Designers may create web pages for stores or companies that want

Web designers arrange the elements for web pages on the Internet.

to sell their products. Designers also may create web pages for art galleries that want to show artwork.

Web pages need to be well organized. Directions must be simple and easy to understand. Pages may be interactive. These pages let users steer through them by controlling and moving the images. Graphic designers must understand what Internet users want on the web sites. This knowledge will help designers create useful web pages.

Tools and Software

Graphic designers may use computer software programs to create graphics or original art. Software programs allow designers to create different effects. Some programs can make images look far away or close up. Others can make certain objects stand out against other design elements. Web page designers can switch and blend colors. They can draw a variety of shapes, lines, and patterns using computer software.

Graphic designers also use tools to create artwork. Some of this art is done with a computer mouse. Other designers use digital tablets. A digital tablet has a special type of mouse.

Graphic designers also use traditional art tools to create some of their art. For example, they use colored pens and pencils to make mock-ups and other drawings.

Publication Designers
Publication designers create layouts for books, magazines, and newspapers. They must be familiar with the readers of their publications.

Web Page Designers
Web page designers design graphics for web pages. They must understand how to attract Internet users to web sites. They need a thorough knowledge of computers and computer programs.

Advertising Designers
Advertising designers design advertisements for clients. They must know their clients' purposes. These designers must understand the target audiences. They should be aware of styles and trends.

Packaging Designers
Packaging designers create packages for a variety of products. They must know the target audiences. They also must know competitors' products.

Chapter 3

The Right Candidate

Graphic designers need a variety of skills. They need to work well with art concepts such as composition, style, and design. Designers need to be observant. They must look at detailed layouts to determine if everything is correct.

Skills and Abilities

Graphic designers need a combination of skills and abilities. Designers must be creative and have good imaginations. They need the ability to judge colors, shapes, widths, and lengths. They should be able to imagine how finished products will look. They must be creative. They need to put ideas together in unique ways.

Graphic designers must have good computer skills. They also must know how to use different

Graphic designers need art skills.

layout programs. This knowledge allows graphic designers to create different types of designs and effects. Designers also should know different word processing programs. Designers may write letters or reports on computers.

Graphic designers should have good math skills. They must be able to take exact measurements and solve math problems. They also should understand advanced forms of math such as algebra and geometry. Designers may use these math skills to draw angles and other designs.

Graphic designers need good organizational skills. They may work on several projects at one time. They must pace their work to meet their project deadlines.

Graphic designers must communicate well. They need to share their ideas with clients, design team members, and other co-workers. Designers must be good listeners. They need to be able to understand directions.

Graphic designers must work well with others.

Designers also must have good writing skills. Some designers may write business letters and reports.

Other Abilities

Graphic designers must be able to work with all types of people. This ability helps designers keep clients. Graphic designers must work well with others. Each client has a different

Skills

Workplace Skills
Yes / No

Resources:
Assign use of time . . . . ✓ ☐
Assign use of money . . . . ✓ ☐
Assign use of material and facility resources . . . . . ✓ ☐
Assign use of human resources . . . . ✓ ☐

Interpersonal Skills:
Take part as a member of a team . . . . ✓ ☐
Teach others . . . . ✓ ☐
Serve clients/customers . . . . ✓ ☐
Show leadership . . . . ✓ ☐
Work with others to arrive at a decision . . . . . ✓ ☐
Work with a variety of people . . . . ✓ ☐

Information:
Acquire and judge information . . . . ✓ ☐
Understand and follow legal requirements . . . . . ✓ ☐
Organize and maintain information . . . . . . ✓ ☐
Understand and communicate information . . . . . ✓ ☐
Use computers to process information . . . . . . ✓ ☐

Systems:
Identify, understand, and work with systems . . . . . ✓ ☐
Understand environmental, social, political, economic,
    or business systems . . . . ✓ ☐
Oversee and correct system performance . . . . . ☐ ✓
Improve and create systems . . . . ☐ ✓

Technology:
Select technology . . . . ✓ ☐
Apply technology to task . . . . ✓ ☐
Maintain and troubleshoot technology . . . . . . ✓ ☐

Foundation Skills

Basic Skills:
Read . . . . ✓ ☐
Write . . . . ✓ ☐
Do arithmetic and math . . . . ✓ ☐
Speak and listen . . . . ✓ ☐

Thinking Skills:
Learn . . . . ✓ ☐
Reason . . . . ✓ ☐
Think creatively . . . . ✓ ☐
Make decisions . . . . ✓ ☐
Solve problems . . . . ✓ ☐

Personal Qualities:
Take individual responsibility . . . . ✓ ☐
Have self-esteem and self-management . . . . . ✓ ☐
Be sociable . . . . ✓ ☐
Be fair, honest, and sincere . . . . ✓ ☐

personality. Some people are easier to work with than others. Graphic designers also must work well with other designers and co-workers.

Graphic designers often work closely with others on projects. This may include sharing office or studio space. Designers must focus on their projects. They need to take directions and work under pressure.

Graphic designers must understand and research current design and advertising trends and styles. Designers need to discover what people like and dislike.

Freelance graphic designers also need business skills. They must order supplies and pay their bills. These designers also may hire assistants to help them on projects. Freelance designers may need to keep payroll or tax records for their employees. Freelance graphic designers also need to keep other business records.

Chapter 4

Preparing for the Career

Students who want to become graphic designers can start to prepare in high school. A variety of classes and activities helps students prepare for careers as graphic designers.

High School Education

Students who want to become graphic designers should take basic art courses in high school. These classes include topics such as color, composition, design, drawing, and layout.

Graphic designers need computer knowledge. Students should take computer classes to learn basic computer skills and computer art skills. Students also should learn desktop publishing skills.

Students learn computer skills and computer art skills in computer classes.

Other classes also may be useful. Mechanical drawing and drafting classes teach students how to make machine designs. Math and geometry classes provide students with skills that are helpful in designing layouts. Students can learn how to understand and communicate with others in English and communication classes.

Volunteer Work and Activities
High school students can benefit from activities outside the classroom. Students can work on school yearbooks or newspapers. They can make posters for school or community events. Students also can volunteer to design signs and charts for day care centers or libraries. People who volunteer to do something are not paid for their work.

Students also may work at design or publishing businesses. This gives students the opportunity to observe professionals working in the field.

Post-Secondary Education
People who want to become graphic designers need formal training to acquire the necessary skills. Some designers earn an associate's degree or college diploma. People earn an associate's degree from a technical or vocational school. In Canada, people earn a college diploma from a

Students can work on school yearbooks or newspapers to gain experience.

community college. Most students finish this degree in about two years.

Other people earn a Bachelor of Fine Arts degree. People earn a bachelor's degree by completing a course of study at a college or university. Most people finish this degree in about four years. Many employers prefer that designers have a Bachelor of Fine Arts degree.

People who want to become graphic designers need formal training.

Many employers want to hire experienced designers. Students may serve internships to gain experience. During internships, students work for professionals in the field. Internships help students learn about graphic design positions. Most interns are not paid for their work.

Registered Designers
In Canada, some graphic designers may become registered. The Ontario provincial government

has given graphic designers professional status. Students must pass the Registered Graphic Designers Qualification Examination after they graduate from school. The Examination Board for Registered Graphic Designers gives the test.

After they pass the test, graphic designers may use the title Registered Graphic Designer (RGD). The Association of Registered Graphic Designers of Ontario oversees graphic designers in Ontario. It also establishes, promotes, and governs uniform standards of knowledge and skill for graphic designers.

The Portfolio

Graphic designers use portfolios to get new jobs. These books or folders contain samples of designers' work. Designers often include different types of art and design in their portfolios. Clients and employers judge designers' skills based on their portfolios. Students can create their portfolios as they develop their art skills.

Graphic designers can learn what employers like by showing their portfolios. They discover what art features appeal to different groups of people. This can help designers decide what type of designs to create.

Chapter 5

The Market

Many job opportunities exist for graphic designers. Growth in the economy creates jobs in all areas of design. The need to spread information provides job opportunities for publishing designers. Businesses' use of the Internet also creates job opportunities for web designers.

Salary

Graphic designers' salaries vary depending on their experience. In the United States, designers earn between $14,560 and $110,000. The average salary for graphic designers in the United States is about $34,000 per year. In Canada, designers earn between $14,500 and $100,000. The average salary for graphic designers in Canada is about $40,000 each year.

Many businesses need graphic designers to help spread information.

Freelance graphic designers' salaries vary the most. Experienced freelance designers make more than beginning freelancers. Freelancers must spend money promoting themselves. But they may spend less on promotion and advertising as they become well known.

Graphic designers usually receive benefits from their employers in addition to their salaries. These benefits include paid health insurance, vacation, and sick time. Designers also may be able to participate in retirement programs.

Job Outlook

In the United States, the job market for graphic designers is expected to grow faster than average. But designers will have competition for available jobs. Many people are entering the field. Graphic designers whose portfolios show artistic skills and creative talent have the greatest job opportunities.

In Canada, the job market for graphic designers is good. There is a large potential for jobs in the field. Graphic designers may have the most opportunities in web design.

Advancement

Graphic designers can advance in their careers as they gain experience and improve their skills.

Graphic designers can advance as they gain experience.

Some designers in large firms may oversee the work of assistants. These people perform duties assigned by designers. Experienced and skilled designers may become chief designers or design department heads. These people oversee the work of designers and assistants.

Graphic designers will continue to be needed in the future. Companies and organizations need ways to share information with the public. Designers are needed to create interesting or new ways to share that information.

Words to Know

brochure (broh-SHUR)—a booklet that gives information about products or services; a brochure usually contains graphics.

client (KLYE-uhnt)—a person or business who uses the services of a professional person such as a graphic designer

copy (KOP-ee)—text used in publications and advertisements

copywriter (KOP-ee-rite-ur)—a person who writes text used in advertisements

freelancer (FREE-lanss-ur)—a person who earns a living independently; a freelancer is paid for individual jobs and does not work for a single business or company.

graphic (GRAF-ik)—a visual image such as an illustration, photograph, or work of art

internship (IN-turn-ship)—a temporary job in which a person works with and learns from skilled workers; college students usually do internships as part of their college program.

layout (LAY-out)—the pattern or design of a page or product; a layout may include text and artwork.

mock-up (MOK-uhp)—a full-size example of a proposed design; graphic designers create mock-ups to show their ideas to clients.

portfolio (port-FOH-lee-oh)—a set of pictures or designs either bound in book form or loose in a folder; graphic designers collect samples of their work in their portfolios.

trend (TREND)—the direction in which things such as styles or ideas are changing

To Learn More

Coleman, LiPuma, Segal & Morrill. *Package Design & Brand Identity: 38 Case Studies of Strategic Imagery for the Marketplace.* Rockport, Mass.: Rockport Publishers, 1994.

Cosgrove, Holli, ed. *Career Discovery Encyclopedia.* Vol. 4. Chicago: Ferguson Publishing, 2000.

Martin, Teresa A., and Glenn Davis. *The Project Cool Guide to HTML.* New York: J. Wiley & Sons, 1997.

Reeves, Diane Lindsey. *Art.* Career Ideas for Kids Who Like. New York: Facts on File, 1998.

Steinhauser, Peggy L. *Mousetracks: A Kid's Computer Idea Book.* Berkeley, Calif.: Tricycle Press, 1997.

Useful Addresses

American Center for Design
325 West Huron Street
Suite 711
Chicago, IL 60610

American Institute of Graphic Arts
164 Fifth Avenue
New York, NY 10010

Society of Graphic Designers of Canada
National Secretariat
Artscourt, 2 Daly Avenue
Ottawa, ON K1N 6E2
Canada

The Society of Publication Designs
60 East 42nd Street
Suite 721
New York, NY 10165

Internet Sites

American Institute of Graphic Arts
http://www.aiga.org

Career Awareness—Graphic Designer
http://www.hrdc-drhc.gc.ca/career/
    directions98/eng/graphic.shtml

Human Resource Development Canada
    Creative Designers and Craftpersons
http://www.hrdc-drhc.gc.ca/JobFutures/english/
    volume1/524/524.htm

Occupational Outlook Handbook—Designers
http://www.bls.gov/oco/ocos090.htm

Society of Graphic Designers of Canada
http://www.gdc.net

Index